Encouraged to Empower

The Coin Flips Once More

Dr. Denise M. Payton

GLO Publications

New Jersey, USA

Printed in America

Encouraged to Empower: The Coin Flips Once More.

All scripture references are taken from the Authorized King James Version, unless otherwise noted.

GLO GLOWS books may be ordered through booksellers; bulk orders may be fulfilled by contacting the author or the publisher: GLO Publications, gloinc2015@gmail.com,(301) 825-6530.

ISBN: 979-8- 9940724-0-0

BIO26000 OCC011020 OCCO19000

DEDICATION

To every woman who ever doubted her worth, every voice that's been silenced by pain, and every heart that's still learning to believe again — this book is for you.

To my daughter, Jarae — your resilience, compassion, and quiet strength inspire me daily. You remind me that empowerment is often found in gentle determination and grace under pressure.

To my son, Jared — your strength, your music, and your faith are living proof that God keeps His promises.

And above all, to God — the lifter of my head, the keeper of my soul, and the Author of every word written on these pages.

TABLE OF CONTENTS

Introduction

When I began writing again, I wasn't sure what I had left to say. The world had changed, and so had I. Between the pages of my first book and the start of this one, I experienced seasons of silence, shifts in identity, and soul-deep growth that I never expected.

This is not a continuation for the sake of storytelling. It's a continuation because God wasn't done — and neither was I.

Introduction Continued

Encouraged to Empower: The Coin Flips Once More was written in the aftermath of fire, the echoes of waiting rooms, and the quiet spaces where God whispers, *"You're still called."*

This is for those who have survived more than they speak about.

For the encouragers who secretly need encouragement.
For the strong ones learning to rest.
For the silent ones ready to speak again.
Each chapter is a coin flip — another layer of discovery, pain, healing, and power.

It is my prayer that these words give voice to your journey and courage to your calling.

You have been through enough.
Now, it's time to rise with intention.
Let us begin — not with fear,
but with faith

Chapter 1
A New Dawn

Chapter 1: A New Dawn

"But those who hope in the Lord will renew their strength. They will soar on wings like eagles; they will run and not grow weary, they will walk and not be faint."— Isaiah 40:31 (NIV)

There's something sacred about a new dawn, the way light slowly stretches across the darkness, reminding us that night doesn't last forever. That hope, when rooted in God, truly has the power to restore, renew, and realign.

Since writing Discouraged to Encourage: And the Coin Flips Again, my life has taken its own series of unexpected flips. I had plans—great, heartfelt plans—to share my message, speak life into others walking the same tightrope of discouragement, and to walk with them toward the light. But as quickly as I released the book, the world shut down.

COVID-19 swept through every corner of our lives, and just like that, we were all sent to homes with fear in our hearts and uncertainty on every screen. I watched the news every day, nervously counting the numbers, mourning for strangers and friends, and thanking God for every breath I still had. I didn't get to share the message like I'd envisioned, but God still had me here—so I knew there was more to come.

During that isolating season, I contracted the virus, not once, but twice. And yet, God brought me through both times. I was afraid, masked, gloved, distant, and cautious. Only my children entered my home. It was a lonely time, but my faith never left me. In fact, that solitude forced me to confront something deeper: Was I truly living, or merely existing?

That question shook me.

I had spent so many years working, serving, pushing forward, always appearing strong. But behind closed doors, in the quiet corners of my room, I had my moments. Tears fell. Doubt crept in. I questioned myself—not my belief in God, but in *me*. Could I still inspire? Could I still trust my own strength?

The answer came quietly but powerfully: "**Yes. Because God made me strong**."

Still, even strong people need somewhere to lean. And sometimes the ones who carry others forget how to be carried themselves.

Faith, I've learned, is not the absence of fear—it's trusting God in the middle of it. Even when I thought my faith was fragile, it was holding me up. God reminded me that He hadn't failed me before, and He wouldn't start now. I simply needed to believe and stay close to His will.

But even with faith, there was a longing I couldn't shake. Not for fame or fortune, but for *connection*. For *companionship*. And that's when the coin flipped again—this time in a way I never expected.

After over 25 years of being alone, I had finally decided it was time to retire, to breathe, to maybe even open my heart again. But with that shift came a vulnerability I didn't anticipate. The enemy, always watchful, used that very longing as an opening.

Someone came into my life—charming, attentive, seemingly God-sent. And for a brief moment, I thought, *maybe this is the love I've waited for*. But it wasn't. Instead, it was a lesson—***wrapped in emotion, covered in confusion, and soaked in heartbreak***.

I had built walls around my heart so high I thought they were unbreakable. Yet one person's attention showed me just how fragile I still was. I questioned everything, my worth, my discernment, my strength. How could I, after all these years, still be so easily wounded?

But then, the revelation came: I had prayed for a companion… ***but I wasn't specific. I asked for someone to walk with, but not someone serious about walking with me. And in that vagueness, I welcomed a distraction that looked like love***

but was sent to derail me. It was a counterfeit sent to detour my purpose.

That experience reminded me that even in our desire for connection, we must be vigilant. Not every presence in our life is a blessing—some are assignments from the enemy to test our stability, our faith, and our identity.

Still, God wastes nothing.

What was meant to break me only revealed the places still in need of healing. What felt like a setback became a setup for reflection, clarity, and ultimately—empowerment.

Through it all, I realized that empowerment doesn't come from pretending we're unshakable. It comes from being honest about our wounds and letting God be our strength in weakness. It comes from knowing who we are in Him, even when others try to make us forget.

The Empowerment of Faith

Empowerment that flows from faith is not loud or boastful. It is quiet, steady, and deeply rooted. It shows up in different ways:

- Inner Peace and Confidence: The calm that comes from knowing God is in control, even when life feels out of control.

- Purpose and Direction: Clarity that cuts through chaos, reminding us why we're here.
- Resilience in Adversity: The bounce-back power that makes the enemy nervous.

- Moral and Ethical Grounding: A compass that keeps us aligned when temptations arise.
- Community and Belonging: The strength of knowing we're not alone.

- Personal Growth: The transformation that makes us wiser, gentler, and stronger.
- Empowering Prayer and Worship: The spiritual fuel that reconnects us to our Source.
- Hope and Optimism: A refusal to give up, even when giving up seems easier.

As I step into this next season of life, I do so with eyes wide open, heart guarded by grace, and purpose firmly planted in faith. I have learned that empowerment is not a moment—it's a mindset. A way of life. And yes, the coin may flip again. But now, I'm ready for whatever side it lands on.**

Welcome to a NEW DAWN.

Let's walk this path—encouraged, empowered, and unafraid.

Reflection: "Waiting to Rise" Sometimes God calls us to pause so He can prepare us for something greater. What felt like a delay was actually divine alignment.

Ask Yourself:

- Where is God calling me to be still?
- How has He used silence to grow me?

Prayer: Lord, thank You for new beginnings. Thank You for reminding me that stillness is not punishment, but preparation. Teach me to wait with expectancy. Renew my strength and awaken my voice once more. In You, I rise. Amen.

CHAPTER TWO

THE RIPPLE EFFECT

Chapter 2: The Ripple Effect

"Let us consider how we may spur one another on toward love and good deeds."— Hebrews 10:24 (NIV)

Empowerment rarely begins and ends with just one person. When God plants something in you—a word, a testimony, a breakthrough—it's never meant to stay bottled up. Encouragement is meant to flow. And when it does, it creates a ripple effect that reaches farther than you could ever imagine.

I want to tell you about someone whose journey reminded me why this work, this calling, and this path toward empowerment is so essential.

Her name was *Danielle*—a quiet spirit with eyes that told stories long before she ever spoke a word. I met her in the early days after my first book release, right before the world shut down. She was a reader, a seeker, and someone carrying the weight of discouragement so quietly it almost

went unnoticed. But God has a way of helping you *see* people when you've walked the path they're silently treading.

We spoke over the phone first. She had read *Discouraged to Encourage* and said something that stopped me in my tracks:

"You made me feel like I wasn't broken beyond repair. Like I still had something worth giving."

That's the moment I realized this was bigger than a book. It was ministry in motion.

Danielle had gone through a difficult divorce, lost her job, and was caring for a sick parent. She had once been bold in her faith—leading worship, mentoring younger women, and teaching Bible study—but life had knocked the wind out of her. She said she no longer recognized the woman in the mirror.

But here's the beauty of God's timing: Just when Danielle thought she was done, God used my *discouragement* to *encourage* her. And through that encouragement, *she began to rise again.*

We stayed in touch—sharing scriptures, prayers, tears, and even laughter.

Slowly, I watched her transformation unfold. She began volunteering again. She started journaling her prayers. She found her voice in small ways, then larger ones. And before long, she was mentoring a group of young women in her church, just as she once had.

She told me months later:

"You didn't fix me, but you reminded me that God still could. You reminded me that I was still useful in His hands."

That moment lit a fire in me. *This* is what empowerment looks like—one life igniting another.

And it made me reflect: how many others are out there like Danielle? How many people just need a word, a reminder, a gentle push back toward purpose?

Empowerment Is Contagious

Danielle's story is not unique. It's *universal.* Encouragement is the seed, but empowerment is the fruit. And that fruit often feeds others. When we rise, we create space for others to do the same.

That's why this new chapter—this new season—is about more than what I've been through. It's about what I can pour out. Because the oil that flows from our pain can become the balm that heals someone else.

If you're reading this and you feel like you're barely hanging on—know this: God isn't finished with you. You may be tired. You may have failed. You may feel unseen. But you are *not forgotten*. And your story still holds power.

When you choose to keep going, even with shaking hands and a heavy heart, you give someone else permission to do the same. That's what Danielle taught me. That's what *God* reminds me, over and over again.

Your Turn to Ripple

Take a moment and think—who in your life could use a word of encouragement? A reminder that God sees them? That strength can return, and hope can rise again?

You don't need a platform. You don't need a stage. You just need willingness.

Empowerment doesn't always come in thunder—it often arrives in whispers, in gentle texts, in silent prayers, in kind gestures. Be someone's ripple today. And watch how God multiplies what you give.

We'll continue this journey together. But as you step into the next chapter, know this: **someone is watching you rise.** And because of your rise, *they just might rise too.*

Reflection: "When Shifting Feels Like Shattering" Too often we mistake divine transitions for spiritual abandonment. But shifting isn't breaking — it's God's method of realignment.

Ask Yourself:

- Am I resisting the shift because of fear?
- What would happen if I stopped clinging to old patterns?

Prayer: Lord, help me to trust You even when I don't understand the process. When my life begins to shift, anchor my faith in Your unchanging hand. Let me not resist but release. In this new season, I don't just want to survive the shift, I want to thrive through it. Amen.

CHAPTER 3
EMPOWERED
IN THE WAITING

Chapter 3: Empowered in the Waiting

"To whom much is given, much will be required."— Luke 12:48 (NKJV)

Leadership is often seen as strength, confidence, and clarity. But what they don't tell you is this: true leadership also requires vulnerability. It means showing up when you feel like staying hidden. It means giving even when you feel empty. It means leading—even while you're still leaning on God for strength yourself.

There have been many seasons in my life when people looked to me for guidance—students, congregants, choir members, mentees, family. I've worn many hats: educator, minister of music, mother, mentor, friend. And in each of these roles, I've done my best to serve with excellence, to give love freely, and to lead with integrity.

But what most didn't see—what I rarely let anyone see—were the moments when I wasn't sure I had anything left to give.

There were days I stood in front of a classroom with tears still drying on my cheeks from the night before. Moments when I led worship while silently wrestling with grief, betrayal, or heartbreak. Times I mentored others while silently longing for someone to pour into me.

That's the paradox of strong people. We pour, and pour, and pour—until one day, we realize the pitcher is nearly empty. But instead of asking for help, we tell ourselves: *Just a little more. They're counting on me. I can't let them see me weak.*

But here's what God began to show me: **Even leaders need a leaning post.**

Reflection: "God, I'm Tired" Courage doesn't mean we never get tired; it means we know where to draw strength.

If your courage feels thin, you're in the perfect position to lean on God's everlasting arms.

Ask Yourself:

- Where in my life do I need divine courage?

- Am I giving myself permission to feel, rest, and recharge?

Prayer: God, I admit I'm tired. Sometimes courage escapes me. But I know You are my strength. Reignite the fire in my heart. Restore what's been depleted. Let me rise again — not in my own power, but in Yours. Amen

The Grace to Be Human

In my solitude, I would often sit quietly before God and just *breathe*. No songs, no fancy prayers—just honesty.

"Lord, I don't know what to do right now. I don't know how to lead through this. I need You to carry me."

And in those still moments, He reminded me: *You were never meant to carry it alone.*

We are not empowered because we are perfect. We are empowered because we are *dependent*—on the One who strengthens us daily. There is grace in being human. There is freedom in acknowledging your limits. And there is power in leading, not from a pedestal, but from a place of *truth*.

People don't need polished leaders—they need *real* ones. Ones who have scars and stories. Ones who admit, "I've been there, too." That's where true connection happens. That's where hearts are changed.

Legacy Beyond Titles

When I think of empowerment, I don't just think of platforms or public praise. I think of **legacy**—the kind that lingers long after the microphone is off and the lights go down.
Legacy is in the way you show up for your children. It's in the way you handle conflict with grace.It's in how you pour wisdom into someone half your age. It's in how you apologize when you're wrong.It's in thc way you serve even when no one sees it.

I want to leave behind more than just accomplishments. I want to leave behind impact. I want those who come behind me to say, "She didn't just lead us—she *loved* us. She didn't just speak truth—she *lived* it."And for **that** to happen, I have to keep growing. Keep healing. Keep surrendering my own ideas of strength and letting God re-define what power really looks like.

Empowered to Lead Differently

Leadership is not about having all the answers. It's about walking in obedience, showing up authentically, and creating space for others to rise.

HERE ARE A FEW TRUTHS I'VE LEARNED ABOUT <u>EMPOWERED LEADERSHIP:</u>

1. **LEAD FROM YOUR STORY, NOT YOUR STATUS.**
People relate to what's real, not what's rehearsed.

2. **MODEL GRACE.**
Be the example of how to fall and get back up with dignity.

3. **LIFT AS YOU CLIMB.**
As you rise, reach back, and bring someone with you.

4. **KNOW WHEN TO REST.**
Rest is not laziness—it's obedience. Even God rested.

5. **STAY TEACHABLE.**
No matter how much you've done, always be open to learn.

6. **PRAY MORE THAN YOU PERFORM.**
Let your **<u>private devotion fuel</u>** your public impact.

Empowerment is not about *being invincible*—it's about *being* ***intentional***. **It's about knowing who you are in Christ**, even when everything around you is uncertain. And it's about recognizing that your ability to lead others begins with your willingness to lean on Him.

So I continue to lead—but now I lead differently. I lead with softness, with honesty, and with an open hand. I lead with a heart that still gets weary, but a spirit that refuses to quit. I lead not because I'm strong every day, but because God's strength never fails.

And if you, too, have been called to lead in your family, your ministry, your community, your field—know this:

You don't have to have it all together to be used by God. You just have to say yes.

Reflection: "There's Power in the Pause" God uses the pause to refine your heart, rebuild your strength, and realign your vision.

Ask Yourself:

- What is God teaching me in this waiting season?
- How can I worship while I wait?

<u>Prayer</u>: Lord, thank You for the waiting seasons — even when they're uncomfortable. Remind me that Your timing is perfect. Give me peace in the pause and wisdom in the stillness. While I wait, I will worship. While I wait, I will walk in faith. Amen.

CHAPTER 4
LEGACY IN
THE BLOODLINE

Chapter 4- Legacy in the Bloodline

"But as for me and my household, we will serve the Lord."— Joshua 24:15 (NIV)

Legacy is not just what you leave behind—it's what you live out loud, day by day, in front of those who watch you the most. And no one watches more closely than your family.

I've always known that the calling on my life wasn't just for me. It was generational. It was rooted in the prayers of those who came before me and reflected in the eyes of those who came after. What I choose to carry—or cast off—echoes into the lives of my children and grandchildren, whether they realize it or not.

We often think of inheritance in material terms—land, finances, property. But the greatest inheritance we can offer is **faith, wisdom, resilience, and love**. A legacy built on godly principles is one that can't be stolen, burned, or devalued. It grows even in the hardest soil.

The Weight and Wonder of Motherhood

Being a mother has been one of the most challenging and rewarding roles of my life. I've had to be the nurturer and the disciplinarian, the safe place and the standard-bearer. There were moments I worried I wasn't getting it right—when I wondered if the sacrifices were noticed, if the lessons were landing, if the love was enough.

But I now understand that even in our imperfections, God covers the gaps. And when you lead your family with love, prayer, and integrity, **something takes root**.

I've watched my children walk through storms I couldn't shield them from, make decisions I prayed they'd avoid, and rise stronger than I could've imagined. It hasn't been a perfect journey—but it's been a faithful one.

What I see now is the power of **generational empowerment**—watching seeds I sowed in tears begin to bloom in the lives of those I love most. They carry their own stories, their own struggles, but I see in them glimpses of the strength I had to fight for. And that brings me peace.**

Honoring Those Who Came Before

My strength didn't begin with me. I come from a lineage of quiet warriors—women and men who didn't always have platforms, but had powerful faith. Some worked in fields, others behind desks, some inside sanctuaries—but all lived with purpose.

I carry their grit in my bones. Their prayers still cover me.

There's something holy about knowing your place in a larger story—about honoring your roots without being bound by them. I've broken some cycles, but I've also continued some sacred traditions: prayer in the morning,

kindness to strangers, wisdom passed over dinner tables, hymns hummed in the kitchen.

Empowerment is inherited. And when it's rooted in faith, it multiplies.

Building a Living Legacy

Now, as I step into this new chapter of my own life, I'm more focused than ever on what I'm *building*, not just what I'm leaving. I want my legacy to be more than photos and possessions. I want it to be:

- **Faith that lives on in every prayer they pray.**
- **Strength that rises in every moment they feel like giving up.**
- **Integrity that guides them when no one else is watching.**
- **Love that's unconditional and unforgettable.**

I want them to remember not just what I did, but who I *was* when no one was watching. I want them to say, "She was real. She walked with God. And she didn't just survive—she helped others live."

And it's not just for my biological family. God has placed spiritual sons and daughters in my path—people I've mentored, prayed for, encouraged. My words matter. My walk matters. My legacy extends through every life I touch.

You Are a Bridge

If you're reading this and wondering where you fit into your family's story, let me tell you: **you are a bridge**.

You may be the first to break a cycle. You may be the only one who believes in healing. You may be the one who builds something new from ground that's never been tilled before.

Don't be discouraged if your legacy-building feels slow or lonely. That's how foundations are laid—quietly, carefully, with intention.

And when your children or your community look back one day, they'll say, "That's where it changed. That's where we started to rise."**

As the coin flips once more, I understand this with clarity: Empowerment is not just ***for*** me—it's ***through*** me***. For my family. For future generations*****.** ***For the ones who come behind me that I may never meet.***

And for you.

You are part of this story now. You are being equipped to leave a legacy of light.

Let's keep building it—together.

Reflection: "God, I'm Tired" Courage doesn't mean we never get tired; it means we know where to draw strength. If your courage feels thin, you're in the perfect position to lean on God's everlasting arms.**

Ask Yourself:

- Where in my life do I need divine courage?
- Am I giving myself permission to feel, rest, and recharge?**

Prayer: God, I admit I'm tired. Sometimes courage escapes me. But I know You are my strength. Reignite the fire in my heart. Restore what's been depleted. Let me rise again — not in my own power, but in Yours. Amen.

CHAPTER 5
HEALING IN
THE HIDDEN PLACES

Chapter 5: Healing in the Hidden Places

"He heals the brokenhearted and binds up their wounds."— Psalm 147:3 (NIV)

Not all wounds are visible. Some are tucked beneath smiles, behind titles, under strength that's been practiced so long it's become a mask. We learn how to keep going. We learn how to speak hope while carrying heartache. But eventually—quietly—we have to face what's still broken.

Healing, I've learned, doesn't always come in a moment. It often comes in layers, in stillness, and in hidden places where no one sees the tears or hears the prayers except God.

I've been through moments that shook me to my core—not just physically, but emotionally and spiritually. I've trusted people who weren't trustworthy. I've given love and received rejection. I've believed promises that were never meant to be kept. And through it all, I had to choose: will I grow *bitter*, or will I grow *better*?

The enemy wants us to believe that betrayal is the end of the story—that failure disqualifies us, or that pain makes us powerless. But I've lived long enough to tell you: **some of the most powerful people are those who have been broken and put back together by God Himself.**

The Danger of Silent Suffering

There's a quiet kind of suffering many of us carry—especially women, especially leaders, especially those who are used to being the "strong one." We convince ourselves that we must keep going, keep serving, keep smiling… because who else will?

But what happens when we can't keep it up anymore?

I remember sitting on the edge of my bed, not long after experiencing what felt like emotional betrayal from someone I deeply cared for. I had believed it was love. I had hoped it was God-ordained. But I was left with silence, confusion, and the weight of my own vulnerability.

And I asked God, not angrily, but honestly:

"Why did I let myself hope again? Why did I open the door—just to be hurt once more?"

His response wasn't immediate. But over time, through prayer and deep soul-searching, I realized: **even disappointment can be divine.** Even closed doors are sometimes answered prayers.

God was protecting me—even from what I thought I wanted.

When God Is Your Counselor

There are seasons when no one can talk you out of your pain—no friend, no sermon, no song. Only God can meet you in that intimate, aching place and begin to restore what life has chipped away.

He sees what no one else does. He hears what you don't even have words for. And He heals in ways that don't always make sense—but always leave you stronger.

There were times when I didn't feel strong. When I doubted if I had anything left to offer. But ***healing reminded me that strength isn't about never being wounded—it's about trusting God to bind the wounds until they become testimonies***.

The Power of Confronting the Pain

Part of healing is honesty.

We have to confront what happened—not to relive it, but to release it. We can't heal what we won't face. And we can't overcome what we're still pretending doesn't hurt.

So I started asking myself real questions:

- *What am I still carrying that God asked me to lay down?*
- *Who am I still trying to prove myself to?*
- *Why do I still feel like I have to be perfect to be loved?*

And little by little, I began to shed the weight of shame, fear, regret, and rejection.

If you're in a place where healing feels far away, let me encourage you: **you are not alone, and you are not beyond repair.** There is no brokenness too deep for God's grace to reach. But you have to be willing to walk through the healing process—even if it's slow.

Healing Is Not Weakness

Sometimes healing is crying when you need to. Sometimes, it's saying "no more" to toxic people or patterns. Sometimes, it's asking for help, or resting, or forgiving—even when there's no apology.

And sometimes, healing is just breathing—deeply, freely, for the first time in a long time.

You don't have to explain your pain to everyone. You don't need validation to begin healing. God already knows. He's already working. And yes, He can use even *this* to bring you closer to your purpose.

I now walk with a peace I didn't have before. Not because everything is perfect—but because I survived what should have broken me. I came through the fire, and I still have my faith. I still have my praise. And I have a deeper empathy for others who are learning how to heal while still hurting.

If that's you—if you're healing in silence—know this:

You are seen. You are loved. And you are healing, even when it doesn't feel like it.

Let the coin flip. Let the process begin. Your healing will not only restore *you*—it will empower *others.*

Because when you come out of this—and you *will*—you'll be a living, breathing testimony that *God is still a healer of broken hearts.*

Reflection: **"Speak, Even If You Tremble "**What have you muted that God wants to magnify? Your voice may be the answer to someone's prayer.

Ask Yourself:

- What fear has kept me silent?
- What truth am I now ready to share?

<u>Prayer</u>: Lord, thank You for the voice You've given me. Help me speak boldly, love deeply, and live authentically. Let my words build bridges and not barriers. I declare today: I will no longer hide. I will speak. Amen.

CHAPTER 6
LIVING
EMPOWERED

Chapter 6: Living Empowered – Everyday Strength for Everyday Life

"For God has not given us a spirit of fear, but of power and of love and of a sound mind."— 2 Timothy 1:7 (NKJV)

Empowerment isn't just a moment—it's a movement. And it's not reserved for platforms, pulpits, or podiums. Real empowerment shows up in the everyday decisions we make, the boundaries we set, the words we speak over ourselves, and the way we carry our God-given identity—even when life tries to strip it away.

After the healing begins, the next step is choosing to live from that place of wholeness. That's where the real journey starts. ***Because healed people empower others***—not by being perfect, but by being present, aware, and intentional about how they move through life.

One of the first areas God restored in me was ***my confidence***—not in people, not in circumstances, ***but in Him within me***. After seasons of being

overlooked, misjudged, or simply surviving, I had to re-learn how to see myself through God's eyes.

That meant no longer shrinking to make others comfortable.

No longer apologizing for being gifted.

No longer disqualifying myself from rooms I was graced to enter.

Confidence is not arrogance. **Confidence is clarity about who you are and *whose* you are**. And when you walk in that kind of identity, you become unshakable—even if your voice trembles at first.

Empowered Confidence—Reclaiming Your Voice

One of the first areas God restored in me was **my confidence**—not in people, not in circumstances, but **in *Him within me***. After seasons of being overlooked, misjudged, or simply surviving, I had to re-learn how to see myself through God's eyes.

That meant no longer shrinking to make others comfortable.

No longer apologizing for being gifted.

No longer disqualifying myself from rooms I was graced to enter.

> Confidence is not arrogance**. Confidence is clarity about who you are and *whose* you are.** And when you walk in that kind of identity, you become unshakable—even if your voice trembles at first.

Empowered Boundaries: Loving Yourself Enough to Say No

God began to show me that *boundaries are not walls to keep others out—they are fences to protect what He's growing in me.*

There was a time when I said "yes" too often—yes to obligations, to draining relationships, to expectations that didn't align with my peace or purpose. And slowly, I felt depleted, misunderstood, even resentful.

But healing taught me how to say *no* with grace. To prioritize peace. To stop explaining myself to people who never intended to understand.

You are allowed to choose your peace.

You are allowed to say "not today" to chaos.

You are allowed to close the door God never asked you to open.

Healthy boundaries are holy. Jesus had them. And so must we.**

Empowered Self-Worth: Knowing You Are Enough

If the enemy can't destroy you, he'll try to convince you that you're not enough.

But hear me clearly: **you are enough because God made you enough.**

Not because of how much you do, Not because of who applauds you,. Not because of perfection.

You are enough simply because God called you His own.

Your value is not up for negotiation. It's not determined by failed relationships, missed opportunities, or mistakes from your past. You are worthy of love. Worthy of joy. Worthy of respect. And worthy of purpose.<u>Say that to yourself until you believe it.</u>

Here are some **practical ways to walk in daily empowerment**:

1. **Start Your Day in God's Presence.** Whether through prayer, scripture, worship, or stillness—center your spirit before the world grabs your attention.
2. **Speak Life—Out Loud.** Affirm who you are in Christ daily. Use declarations that remind your spirit of truth: "*I am loved. I am chosen. I am powerful. I am protected. I am enough.*"
3. **Guard Your Inner Circle.** Surround yourself with people who speak life, not drain it. Choose community that uplifts, holds you accountable, and reflects God's love.
4. **Set One Goal a Day That Serves Your Purpose.**

Empowerment comes through small wins. Each step forward—no matter how small—is movement in the right direction.

5. **Honor Your Yes and Your No.** Let your words match your values. Say yes to what aligns with purpose. Say no to what disrupts your peace.
6. **Celebrate Yourself Without Guilt.** Your growth deserves recognition. Pause and give God thanks for how far you've come—even if you're not yet where you want to be.

7. **Rest When needed.** Empowered people don't burn out to prove themselves. They understand that rest is a weapon.

Walking Empowered Is a Daily Choice

Every day you wake up, you're faced with a choice: will I walk in fear or in faith? Will I respond from wounds or wisdom? Will I shrink back or step forward?

Living empowered doesn't mean every day is easy. It means you face life with courage, covered by grace, led by the Spirit, and grounded in truth.

You don't need to wait for a platform, title, or applause. You are empowered to show up in your own life fully present, fully healed, and fully committed to becoming all that God has called you to be.

So go ahead—speak up. Walk tall. Protect your peace. Trust your healing. Celebrate your growth. And let your life preach the sermon that someone else has been waiting to hear.

Because the coin has flipped once again—and this time, *you're standing in your power.*

Reflection: "Unburned but Refined" The fire was never meant to destroy you — it was meant to purify what you carry.

Ask Yourself:

- What fires have I survived?
- Can I recognize God's presence even in hardship?

Prayer: Lord, thank You for walking with me through every trial. Even when I couldn't feel You, you were there. Refine me, not to harm me, but to make me whole. I trust you with the fire. Amen.

CHAPTER 7
ROOTED
AND READY

Chapter 7: Rooted and Ready—Spiritual Disciplines That Sustain Empowerment

"Blessed is the one...whose delight is in the law of the Lord, and who meditates on his law, day and night. That person is like a tree planted by streams of water, which yields its fruit in season and whose leaf does not wither."— Psalm 1:1–3 (NIV)

Empowerment without spiritual discipline is like a house with no foundation—it might stand for a while, but it won't last when the storms come.

We've talked about rising from discouragement, healing after heartbreak, and walking in daily strength. But now, we must talk about the roots—the habits, the rhythms, and the sacred practices that keep us grounded when life tries to shake us.

Empowered living doesn't just happen. It's cultivated. And the soil in which it grows is spiritual discipline.

1. Prayer: Your Power Source

Prayer is not just talking to God—it's connecting with the very source of your strength. It's where clarity comes. Where burdens are exchanged for peace. Where empowerment is refueled.

You don't need perfect words. Just an open heart.

Some days, my prayers are declarations. Other days, they're whispered cries for help. But every prayer, no matter how simple, draws me closer to God's heart and re-aligns me with His will.

- **Empowered Tip:** Create a prayer routine. Morning prayer centers your day. Evening prayer closes it with peace. Keep a journal to track answered prayers—you'll be amazed at what God does.

2. Worship: A Weapon and a Healing Balm

-
-

-
-
-
-
- Worship is where you remember who God is—and who you are in Him. When life tries to rob you of joy, worship puts it back in your hands.
- Whether through singing, silence, dancing, or devotion, worship softens hardened hearts and lifts weary souls. It reminds you that even in the valley, He is worthy.
- **Empowered Tip:**Set aside time each week for personal worship. Play music, light a candle, or just sit still in His presence. Let your home become a sanctuary.

3. Fasting: Clearing the Clutter

Fasting is not just abstaining from food—**it's *making room* for God**. When you fast, you silence distractions and heighten your spiritual sensitivity.

Some of my most powerful revelations came when I denied myself what I *wanted* so I could receive what I truly *needed*—divine instruction, peace, healing, correction.

- **Empowered Tip:**Start with short fasts—one meal, one day, or from social media or distractions. Let each fast have a focus. Write down what God reveals during those moments of sacrifice.

4. Scripture: Fuel for the Journey

The Word of God is not just a book—it's life. It feeds your faith, strengthens your spirit, and renews your mind.

I cannot count the number of times a verse met me *right where I was*. In grief. In joy. In indecision. In pain.

- **Reading the Bible** isn't a task to check off—**it's an invitation to be transformed.****
- **Empowered Tip:**Choose a daily verse to meditate on. Write it on a sticky note. Speak it aloud. Let it become part of your spiritual DNA. Try reading one Psalm or Proverb a day to start.**

5. Discernment: Hearing the Still, Small Voice

- Empowered people make empowered decisions. And that requires **discernment**—the ability to hear God clearly and separate truth from noise.
- Discernment is developed through stillness, study, and submission. You can't be spiritually sharp when your soul is always in chaos.
- The more time you spend with God, the more easily you'll recognize His voice over the enemy's lies or your own impulses.
- **Empowered Tip:** When faced with a decision, don't rush. Fast. Pray. Listen. Pay attention to what brings peace vs. what brings pressure. God's voice leads with clarity, not confusion.

6. Community: Don't Grow Alone

You weren't meant to do this walk alone. Isolation makes us vulnerable. Accountability and encouragement make us strong.

Spiritual community—whether through a church, small group, prayer partner, or mentor—keeps us grounded. It reminds us we're part of something bigger.

> ➢ **Empowered Tip:** Find your people. Connect with others who challenge you spiritually and cheer for your growth. Let them see the real you—this is where true empowerment multiplies.

When Your Roots Run Deep

Empowerment isn't about being constantly fired up—it's about being **firmly planted**. When your roots run deep in prayer, worship, scripture, and discernment, you won't be easily moved by life's winds.

You'll speak from a place of wisdom. You'll act from a place of peace. You'll pour from a place of overflow.

And when others see you walking in power, they won't just see a strong woman or man—they'll see someone **anchored in God**.

So let this chapter be your reminder: *staying empowered requires staying connected.* Let the disciplines of your spirit become the rhythm of your life.

Because the coin may flip again—but this time, **you're rooted, ready, and unshakable.**

Reflection: **"Boundaries Birth Balance"** Saying no is not rejection — it's re-alignment. It creates space for your divine yes.

Ask Yourself:

- What do I need to release?
- Am I saying yes out of fear or faith?

Prayer:

Lord, teach me the power of divine boundaries. Help me say yes only when You lead and no without guilt. I choose Your alignment over approval. Amen.

CHAPTER 8
GRACE FOR
THE GAPS

Chapter 8: Grace for the Gaps, Testimonies of Triumph—

When Encouragement Sparks Empowerment

"They triumphed over him by the blood of the Lamb and by the word of their testimony..."— Revelation 12:11 (NIV)

There's something deeply powerful about hearing someone say, *"I've been there too."* Testimonies connect us in a way that sermons sometimes can't. They remind us that miracles don't just happen in the Bible—they happen in real life, in real people, in real pain.

In this chapter, I want to share the stories of people whose journeys mirrored the themes of this book: discouragement, surrender, healing, and ultimately, **empowerment**. Some were quietly struggling, others loudly lost. But each of them encountered God through encouragement—and their lives were never the same.

JASMINE: FROM SILENCE TO SONG

Jasmine was once a woman of few words. Life had taught her to be quiet, to not expect much, to settle into shadows. Years of emotional abuse had muted her voice and shrunk her sense of worth. She attended Bible studies but never spoke. She served faithfully but never smiled.

Then one evening during a women's ministry gathering, she was handed a copy of *Discouraged to Encourage*. She said, "I didn't even want to read it—but I heard something say, *'This is for you.'*"

Page after page, something inside her began to rise. She later shared with me, "You gave me the courage to open my mouth again. To believe that my voice was valuable. That I wasn't invisible."

Months later, Jasmine joined the worship team—not as a soloist at first, but as someone willing to stand, sing, and let her voice be heard. Today, she helps lead others in praise. Her silence turned into a song. And she now uses her voice to remind other women: *"You are still here. You still matter."*

VICTOR: THE REBUILT MAN

Victor had served time. He carried the weight of mistakes, guilt, and a broken relationship with his family. He believed that forgiveness was for others—not for people like him.

He read *Discouraged to Encourage* while serving the final months of his sentence through a re-entry mentorship program. A volunteer gave him the book and said, "Just read the first chapter." He did—and kept going.

He told me in a letter:

"Your words gave me hope that I wasn't beyond redemption. I started journaling. Started reading scripture. I began asking God to show me what was left of the man I used to be."

Victor left prison not just rehabilitated—but **renewed**. He now works as a youth mentor for at-risk teens and says, "If I can stop just one young man from making the mistakes I made, then I've done something with this second chance."

Victor isn't just rebuilding his life—he's building *others*.

TERESA: THE QUIET LEADER AWAKENS

Teresa was a woman who did everything for everyone—except herself. A caretaker by nature, she was the first to show up, the last to leave, and never asked for help. But inside, she was exhausted. Empty. Unseen.

She picked up the sequel, *Encouraged to Empower*, at a church retreat. She said something clicked immediately:

"I realized I wasn't just surviving—I was disappearing."

For the first time in years, she stepped back from overcommitment. She sought counseling. She started writing again—a gift she had buried under obligation.

And something beautiful happened: her family noticed. Her joy returned. Her peace deepened. She became more than a helper—she became a **whole woman**.

Today, Teresa leads a monthly prayer group for women who serve others but often forget themselves. She says, *"My healing helped unlock healing in others. That's the power of encouragement."*

Empowerment Is Meant to Be Shared

These stories aren't here to entertain—they're here to remind you: **this message works**. Encouragement is not just kind words—it's a key. A lifeline. A spark that sets off a chain reaction of healing, growth, and boldness.

Each of these individuals found strength through someone else's obedience—someone who spoke, wrote, gave, or showed up. And now *they* are doing the same for others.

That's what empowerment looks like in real time.

WHAT WILL YOUR TESTIMONY BE?

.☛☛☛ Now, the question comes to you.

- Who are you called to encourage?
- Whose life might shift because of your voice, your survival, your obedience?
- What pain have you come through that could become someone else's breakthrough?

You don't need a platform—you need purpose. You don't need perfection—you need willingness.

Your story matters. And whether you share it in a pulpit, across a kitchen table, in a journal, or through your daily actions—***your voice can change a life.***

Because when the coin flips in your favor, don't just celebrate. **Reach back and flip someone else's too.**

Reflection: "I'm Not Perfect, But I'm Covered"

God's strength is most visible in your surrender.

Ask Yourself:

- What area of my life needs grace?
- Am I trying to earn what God has already given?

Prayer: Jesus, thank You for Your sufficient grace. I release my need to perform. Fill the broken spaces with Your love. Let my weakness be a testimony of Your power. Amen

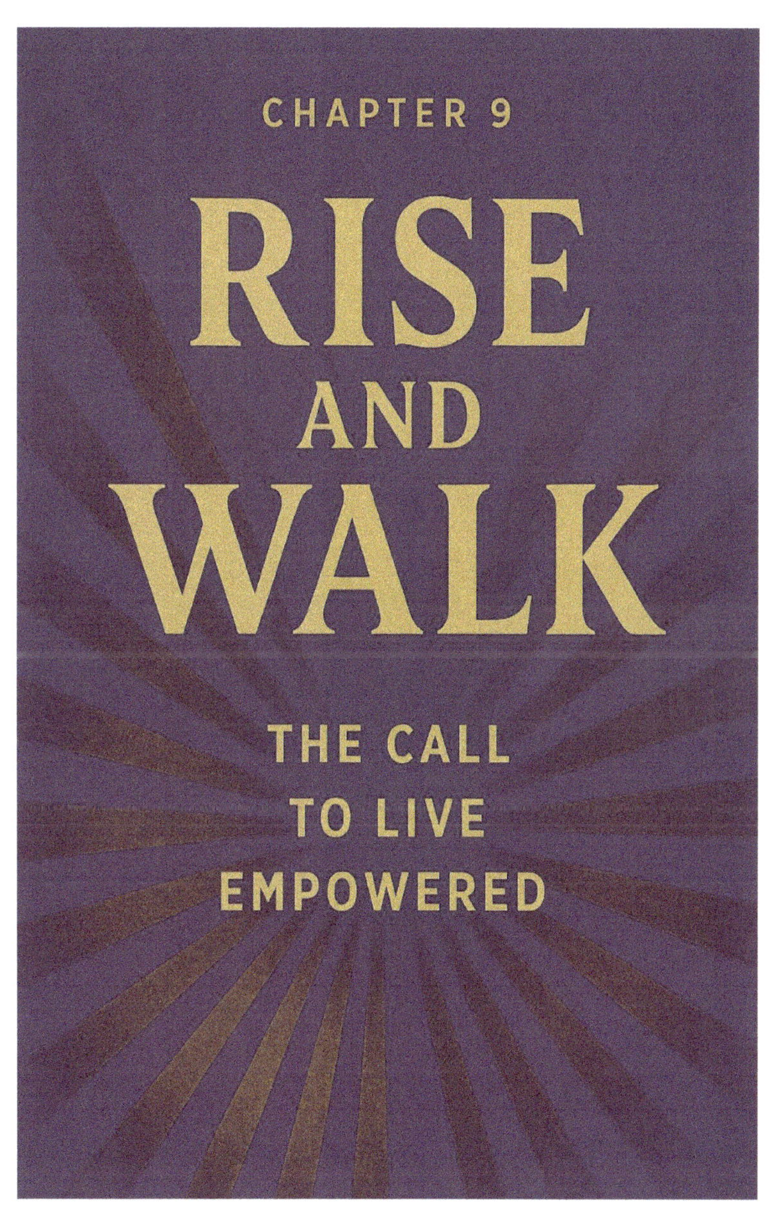
CHAPTER 9
RISE
AND
WALK
THE CALL
TO LIVE
EMPOWERED

Chapter 9: Rise and Walk—The Call to Live Empowered

"Get up! Take your mat and walk."— John 5:8 (NIV)

There comes a moment—after the tears have dried, the healing has begun, and the revelation has come—when we must decide: **Will I stay where I've been, or will I rise and walk in the fullness of who I am?**

You've read the stories. You've reflected on your pain. You've seen how encouragement became the soil for empowerment. And now the coin has flipped once more—not by accident, but by *divine appointment.*

God is calling you to rise.

Not in fear, but in **faith**. Not in timidity, but in **truth**. Not with your head down, but with your **spirit lifted**.

Because **empowered living** is not just a concept—it's a **commission**.

The Journey Has Prepared You

Everything you've endured has built the muscle you didn't know you'd need. The discouragement taught you how to hear God's whisper. The heartbreak revealed the cracks in your foundation, so He could rebuild it. The solitude showed you who you are without applause.

NONE OF IT WAS WASTED.

You've walked through the fire. You've wrestled in the dark. You've wept in silence.

And now, like the man at the pool of Bethesda, Jesus is speaking directly to your soul:

*"**Get up**."*

You're not too broken. You're not too old. You're not too late. You're not too far behind.

The same power that raised Jesus from the grave lives in you—and it's time to walk in it,

Living Empowered Means…

- **Speaking truth** even when your voice shakes.
- **Setting boundaries** that protect your peace and purpose.
- **Choosing joy** when bitterness would be easier.
- **Letting go of what no longer fits where God is taking you**.
- **Encouraging others from a place of authenticity, not perfection**.

You don't have to know the full path. Just take the next faithful step.

You Are the Answer

Someone is awaiting your story. Someone is praying for a word you carry. Someone needs the light you've fought to keep burning.

Your voice, your vision, your presence—it matters.

You are not just being empowered for yourself. You are being empowered **for assignment**. For impact. For legacy. For kingdom purpose.

What you survived wasn't just survival—it was training ground.

Reflection: "From Overcome to Overcomer" You were never meant to keep your strength to yourself.

Ask Yourself:

- Who can I encourage today?
- Where can I plant seeds of empowerment?

Prayer: God, I thank You for every experience that has strengthened me. I now step boldly into the assignment of empowerment. Let my story uplift others. Let my life be a reflection of Your power. Use me, Lord. Amen.

THE FINAL FLIP

As we close this chapter, I want you to imagine the coin flipping one last time. But this time, it doesn't land in uncertainty. It lands in **clarity**.

You are no longer waiting on permission. You are no longer wondering *if* you're ready. You are no longer asking *when* your moment will come.

It's now. It's here. It's you.

A Final Prayer and Commission

Lord, I thank You for every reader who has walked this journey through these pages. I thank You for their scars, their strength, their sacred process. May every lesson bloom into boldness. May every tear water the seeds of their calling. And may they walk, not in fear, but in power, love, and a sound mind .Let them rise and not grow weary. Let them walk and not faint. And let their lives become the encouragement someone else is waiting for. In Jesus' name, Amen.

Now, RISE-—encouraged, empowered, and unstoppable.

THE WORLD IS WAITING. And YOUR TIME IS NOW.,

Bonus—Empowerment Scriptures

Here is a collection of scriptures that have carried me, comforted me, and empowered me in every season. May they do the same for you:

Isaiah 40:31 (NIV) *"But those who hope in the Lord will renew their strength. They will soar on wings like eagles; they will run and not grow weary, they will walk and not be faint."*

Romans 8:28 (NIV) *"And we know that in all things God works for the good of those who love him, who have been called according to his purpose."*

Joshua 1:9 (NIV) *"Have I not commanded you? Be strong and courageous. Do not be afraid; do not be discouraged, for the Lord your God will be with you wherever you go."*

Philippians 4:13 (NIV) *"I can do all this through him who gives me strength."*

2 Corinthians 12:9 (NIV) *"But he said to me, 'My grace is sufficient for you, for my power is made perfect in weakness.'"*

Isaiah 30:18 (NIV) *"Yet the Lord longs to be gracious to you; therefore he will rise up to show you compassion."*

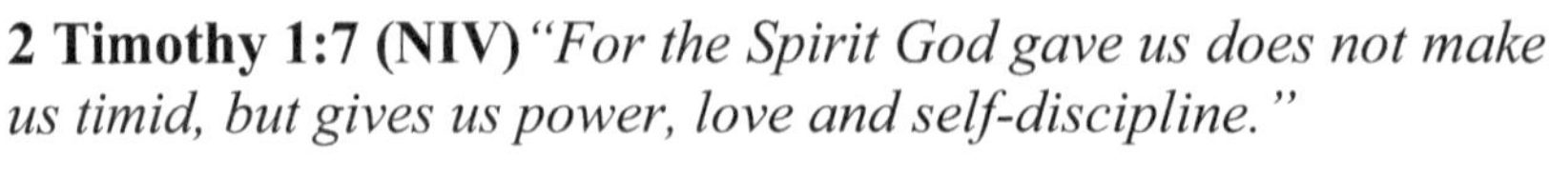

2 Timothy 1:7 (NIV) *"For the Spirit God gave us does not make us timid, but gives us power, love and self-discipline."*

Daniel 3:25 (NIV) *"Look! I see four men walking around in the fire, unbound and unharmed, and the fourth looks like a son of the gods."*

Matthew 5:37 (NIV) *"All you need to say is simply 'Yes' or 'No'; anything beyond this comes from the evil one."*

LET THESE WORDS OF TRUTH BE YOUR ANCHOR, YOUR SWORD, AND YOUR SONG. DECLARE THEM DAILY, AND WALK BOLDLY IN THE EMPOWERMENT GOD HAS ALREADY GIVEN YOU.

A Heartfelt Letter from the Author

Dear Reader,

If you've made it to this page, I want to pause and simply say — thank you. Thank you for taking the time to walk through these pages, these reflections, and these moments of my life that I have so prayerfully shared with you.

This book was not written from a place of perfection, but from the raw and real places where I learned to lean into God. It was born out of seasons where I didn't think I had the strength to write again, to sing again, or even to believe again. But God — He never stopped writing my story. And He certainly hasn't stopped writing yours.

I pray that as you turned each page, you didn't just hear my voice — I pray you heard God's. I hope the scriptures, stories, and prayers encouraged your heart, reminded you of your worth, and reignited your power to rise.

You are not alone. You are not disqualified. And you are certainly not forgotten.

The same God who brought me from discouraged to encouraged, and now from empowered to empowering, is at work in you too. Don't hide your scars. Share your journey. Someone else needs what you carry.

Thank you for allowing me to walk with you — if only for a few chapters.

With all my heart,

Denise Murchison Payton

Dr. Denise Murchison Payton

About the Author

Dr. Denise Murchison Payton is a multifaceted music professional, educator, author, and encourager whose life's mission is to uplift and empower others through faith, testimony, and the transformative power of music. A native of Spring Lake, North Carolina, she has served with distinction as the Director of Choral Activities and Music Area Coordinator at Fayetteville State University, where she led generations of students with excellence, love, and spiritual integrity.

A gifted soprano, voice instructor, and Minister of Music, Dr. Payton has dedicated over four decades to inspiring students, mentoring artists, and cultivating powerful musical experiences. She is known for her passionate leadership, authentic storytelling, and commitment to spiritual growth through education and the arts.

In addition to her professional accomplishments, Dr. Payton is the author of *Discouraged to Encourage: And the Coin Flips Again* and now, this heartfelt sequel, *Encouraged to*

Empower: The Coin Flips Once More. Both works reflect her journey of faith, resilience, and the calling to empower others by sharing her story with transparency and grace.

Now embarking on a new chapter through her brand **Payton Phoenix Rising**, she continues to mentor, teach, and inspire, reminding everyone that their story is not over — and that even after the fire, the phoenix still rises.

To connect or learn more, visit her platform and follow her journey of transformation, faith, and empowerment.

Acknowledgments

To God be all the glory — for every word, every tear, every breakthrough that led to this moment. Thank You for being the Author of my story and the Sustainer of my strength.

To my family, friends, students, and fellow believers who have walked with me through seasons of discouragement and celebration — your love and encouragement made room for this book to exist.

To the readers of *Discouraged to Encourage*, thank you for embracing my first offering. This second one is for you — for everyone who kept flipping the coin and dared to believe again..

To every choir member, workshop attendee, and person I've had the privilege of mentoring, singing with, or teaching — you are forever part of my journey.

And to the women and men who are still in the waiting, still finding their voice, still rebuilding after the fire:

This is your reminder —

You are seen, you are valued, and you are called to rise.

With deepest gratitude,

Dr. Denise Murchison Payton

www.ingramcontent.com/pod-product-compliance
Lightning Source LLC
LaVergne TN
LVHW010618110826
845149LV00003B/961

* 9 7 9 8 9 9 4 0 7 2 4 0 0 *

Time for Healing

LINDA COLLINS-HUGHES

ZOË Life
COACHING • CONSULTING • PUBLISHING

TABLE OF CONTENTS

DEDICATION

This book is dedicated first and foremost to the work of the Lord; to God be the Glory.

To my children: Melissa, LaTonia and Knobert Jr.

To my daughter in love Rashonda; to my grandchildren, Brittany, Kimberlyn, Kayla, Jadon, Jaeda, Tim, Tymia and Jhaidon.

To my grandson in love, Gene; to my great-grandchildren, Stephanie, Tre and Khari.

Also, to the woman that gave birth to me, my mother, Mary Lee Collins Standberry.

I pray that as you read this book, you will become more encouraged to work for the Lord. I am inspired to share with you the thoughts that God has given to me. I pray that these anointed topics which God has given me will help you in whatever your situation may be. These topics are messages of hope. I pray that as you read this book, the anointing will flow from page to page, to the very depth of your soul. As God instructed me on how to present each of these topics, I was truly blessed by His presence. I am encouraged to go on and see what the end is going to be. I know that if you take your time and read these topics and let God minister to your need as He did mine, I believe you will be encouraged. Whatever your concerns, I believe you will find encouragement in these topics!

TRIBUTE

I thank God for my grandfather, the late Elder Tom Collins, and my grandmother, the late Mother Mary Elizabeth James-Collins.

I was raised by these two people that I called *Mother* and *Daddy*. They poured so much into my life as a child, prompting me to be the Woman of God, I've become in such a time as this. I watched them as leaders in church and in their home.

My grandfather was the pastor of Collins Temple and Red Lick C.O.G.I.C. My grandmother was the ideal First Lady. She was meek, humble and Holy. My grandparents were God fearing and trusted in God for all things. They, were loved by all that encountered them. They, one hundred percent believed in living holy. One of their favorite scriptures was Hebrews 12:14, "*Follow peace with all men, and holiness, without which no man shall see the Lord.*" One of his quotes was, "*Follow me as I follow Christ*". They've been gone for such a long time but their legacy lives on. They taught us so much. Proverbs 22:6 says, "*Train up a child in the way he should go and when he is old, he will not depart from it.*"

I thank God for the training. They taught me to work hard, to put God first, and always lead by example.

GONE AND NEVER FORGOTTEN

4/9/1911 --- 1/2/1974

12/22/1914 --- 4/29/1986

INTRODUCTION

DM Erma J. Brent AKA 'Mom Brent'

Time for Healing was birthed during the tenure of our beloved late District Missionary, Erma Jean Brent. She inspired me to drive and go forward. Through the annual *Time for Healing* conferences, I was inspired to continually work for the Lord, inspiring others to do so as well. I thank God for having known Mom Brent. One of her sayings was, "*I may be hopping but I'm not stopping.*" She was an anointed, powerful vessel used by God. Mom Brent was truly a blessing to all that came in contact with her. I pray that the topics in this book will bless your soul and know that God is a healer. If we continue to trust God, we can be healed, delivered and set free.

ABOUT THE AUTHOR

Linda Marie Collins-Hughes

Linda Marie Collins-Hughes is a member of the Gethsemane COGIC under the leadership of Administrative Assistant, Supt. Perry Clark Sr.

Missionary Linda Hughes was appointed the McComb District Missionary in September of 2020 by the late Bishop A.V. Jordan. In ministry, she is the YWCC Jurisdictional president of second southern Mississippi. She serves as the president and founder of the *Time for Healing* Ministry, organized under the late District Missionary Erma Jean Brent.

In 2018 she started a prayer line for her family, which is still going strong today. In June 2021, she graduated from the C.H. Mason Jurisdictional Bible Institute.

Professionally, she is the first black certified surgical first assistant (CSFA) employed by King Daughters Medical Center. She has served there for 29 years. She has been a veteran of the operating room since 1976 (48+yrs.). She started her career at Southwest Medical Center in McComb, MS, (1976-1990) and then continued it at North Oaks Medical Center in Hammond, LA and (1990-1996). Finally, she has served in this position at KDMC in Brookhaven, MS from 1996 to present.

She has also served as Clinical Instructor for the Hinds Community College Surgical Technology Program. She is the Godly proud mother of 3 children, 8 grandchildren and 3 great- grandchildren, but most importantly, she is a *Woman of God*!

MY PRAYER

Father in the mighty name of Jesus, I truly thank you for this day that you have given me, a day you didn't have to let me see but you did, and I just want to say thank you. I thank You for life health and strength. Thank You for new mercies on this day and every day. Thank you, Lord, for my children, grandchildren, great-grandchildren. I thank you for my entire family. Lord, I Thank you for keeping us together. Thank you for allowing me to put these topics together to the Glory and honor of You. Lord, You are my rock, my shield, my deliverer; You are my strength. In You, I put all my trust. I praise You because You are so worthy to be praised. I will bless You at all times and your praise shall continually be in my mouth. I will praise You, Oh Lord with my whole heart. Oh Lord how excellent is Your name in all the Earth. There is none like You nowhere. You are my all in all, my Jehovah Jireh, my EL Shaddai. Help us Lord as we continually look to You for our help, because all our help comes from You, my Lord. Help us to stay focused and to always look to the hills from which our help comes. Lord, we ask you to incline your ear toward us as we call on your sweet Holy Name. We pray for peace in this troubled world. Only You, Lord can give peace. We ask you to speak Lord, show us what to do in these perilous times that we are living in. Only You Lord can help us in these perilous times. Lord, You calmed the raging sea, and I know you can and will calm the situations in this world today. Lord, I realize there is something we must do. You said in Your Word, if we, your people which are called by your name, would humble ourselves and pray, seek Your face and turn from our wicked ways - You said what You would do. You said You would heal, hear, and forgive. Lord, help us to line up to what You would have us to do, realizing that time is winding up, that we are living in the last and evil days. Help us Lord to be ready for your return. Help us Lord because we want to meet You in peace. I pray we all are ready because our endeavor is to hear You say, "*Well done, thy good and faithful servant.*"

These and other blessing we ask in Jesus' Name I pray…. Amen, Amen, Amen!

One

WALK INTO YOUR SEASON

As I began to study seasons, I thought about a special period. As the Lord ministered to me, I could hear Him say, "*This is your time, your period - now walk therein.*"

I was instructed to look at Joseph. So, I went to Genesis 39:1-6 then to Genesis 41:37-42.

Joseph, as we all know, was the eldest son of Jacob by his wife Rachel and the older brother of Benjamin. Joseph also had half-brothers who resented him because of the love their father had for him. You see, Joseph was a good child. You have people that resent you simply because you are good. Joseph was one that was highly favored by God and his father. Joseph had no idea that he was about to embark upon his destiny. He really wasn't aware that he was being set up for a blessing. He didn't realize he was about to walk into *his* season. Those of you that are reading this right now, *Get Ready, Get Ready, Get Ready*. The troubles you went through last year were only a set up; you are about to walk into your season.

As I said earlier, Joseph was a good child and well favored by God and his father. His father thought a lot of him and in the process, he made him a coat of many colors. Well this if you can imagine, really angered his half-brothers. As Joseph was tending sheep with his brothers, some of them did mischievous things; in other words, they were misbehaving. Joseph reported their actions to his father, so you can imagine that this did not sit well with his brothers. I'm sure they probably called him "tattle tell" or "blabbermouth." Remember, these were his half-brothers, so they really didn't care a lot about Joseph as a real brother. We have some half-saints that do the same thing. They will throw rocks and hide their hands because they are not real saints, and don't care a lot about you. Real saints love one another. You see, Joseph had trouble with those half-brothers. He didn't have trouble with Benjamin, his real brother. Joseph basically stayed close to his father and his younger brother Benjamin. His brothers hated him simply because of who he was. There are people today that hate you simply because of who you are. But don't worry about that, it's only a set up. God is getting you in position to receive your blessing. Glory to God!

We know that Joseph was a dreamer, as his brothers called him. Whenever Joseph had a dream, he would tell the dream to his brothers (big mistake), and this really infuriated them. They really couldn't see his dream coming to past. They couldn't see themselves bowing to Joseph. People today are just like this when they see elevation taking place in your life and this is why you can't tell everything God shows you to everybody. Be patient and wait.

Joseph had a dream, one day that he would reign over a people and He would be in a leadership position. God is about to exalt Joseph. When the enemy sees God moving in your life he gets upset and busies himself trying to block your progress. This is what happened in Joseph's case. His brothers hated him, and they knew they did not want Joseph over them. So, they conspired to kill him.

There are people conspiring to get rid of you because of who you are in Christ. Just don't stop working for the Lord, because He has got you back. So, whatever you are going through remember, *you are about to walk into your season.*

Now you see the half-brothers had decided to kill Joseph, but Rueben stopped them. Instead, they sold him into slavery to local Ishmaelites. Then, they tried to cover up their mischievous act by killing an animal and dipping Joseph's coat in animal's blood. They returned the coat to Jacob, wanting him to think that his beloved son had been killed. This was such a devious act. The devil is crazy. The enemy will lie, throw stones, and then try to cover up what he has done; *but* - God sees all. The brothers failed to realize that this was working together for Joseph's good.

Joseph was sold into Egypt as a slave to a man named Potiphar. Now mind you, Joseph was only seventeen at that time. But unknown to him, God was working out a great purpose by this set of circumstances. Joseph was dependable and successful in all he went to do. He was a sound-minded person and very competent. Now Potiphar was observing all these things. <u>So don't you get weary in well doing</u> (Gal. 6:9); God has somebody watching you. In turn, Potiphar placed Joseph over the entire house. Joseph had it going on because God was with him. Whatever he touched God blessed, wherever he was God Blessed. When the enemy see you doing well, he gets stirred up. The enemy stirred against Joseph through Potiphar's wife. She lied on him because he would not submit to her advances. She tried to destroy his character. The enemy will do the same thing to you but keep your integrity intact and keep living for God.

Potiphar believed his wife and had Joseph put in prison. During this time, Joseph went through a lot. He was sold into slavery by his brothers that truly hated him, he was torn away from his father and younger brother whom he loved very much, he was humiliated and thrown into prison - but God was with him all the way. Joseph didn't know it, but he was working toward his destiny. Sometimes it seems as if you are at the bottom of the barrel but hold on, God will see you through. Look at how God molded Joseph into the leader He wanted him to be. You must just hold on and go through.

Let's look at Joseph a little more…

After being put into prison the head jailer recognized Joseph's capabilities and put him in charge of the whole prison. Joseph had wisdom and grace, something that the enemy could not take away with cruelty. He could not be stripped of his virtue and integrity. While Joseph was in prison he made a friend, he thought (remember Genesis 40:14,15,23).

"But think on me when it shall be well with thee, and show kindness, I pray thee, unto me, make mention of me unto Pharoah, and bring me out of this house, for I indeed was stolen away out of the land of the Hebrews: and here also have I done nothing that they should put me into this dungeon".

The chief butler still forgot all about Joseph. Joseph had ministered to him, helped him, and still he was forgotten. People are like that today - it doesn't matter how much you do for them, still when they get on the mountain top (so to speak) they will forget you. Don't you worry about that because God is not asleep - He sees all, and He knows all. Hallelujah!! Joseph was thirty years old when he stood before Pharoah, after being in prison for thirteen years. He finally was able to walk into his season. It doesn't matter how long you must go through your period of molding, just remember that God is with you always. Now hold your head up and go through. Remember there's a song that says, "*Trouble don't last always.*"

Let's look at Genesis 41:37-42…

"and the thing was good in the eyes of Pharoah, and in the eyes of all his servants. And Pharoah said unto his servants, can we find such a one as this, a man in whom the spirit of God is? And Pharoah said unto Joseph. Forasmuch as God hath shown thee all this, there is none so discreet and wise as thou art. Thou shall be over my house, and according unto thy word shall all my people be ruled: only in thy throne will I be greater than thou. And Pharoah said unto Joseph see, I have set thee over all the land of Egypt. And Pharoah took off his ring from his hand, and put it upon Joseph's hand, and arrayed him in vestures of fine linen, and put a gold chain about his neck."

So many of us like Joseph have been pushed aside, humiliated, hated, scorned and even lied on. But we must remember that God is in control. The devil will try to put you in a horrible pit but hold on to your promise. Every promise in the Book is yours - every chapter, every verse, and every line. Keep trusting in God. God said that He would never leave us nor forsake us. He promised that He would be with us always. Glory to God!!! We must understand that we are headed toward our destiny. Don't let people slow you down with their lies. Look at what Potiphar's wife said about Joseph but that lie didn't stop Joseph from walking into his season. People are going to dig ditches but look up you are coming out, just keep looking up to the author and finisher of our faith. It doesn't matter what the enemy says or does, just walk into your season. Satan realizes what God is going to do in your life and that's why he's trying so hard to stop you from taking your rightful place. Satan is afraid of your anointing and is aware of who you are and whose you are. Keep walking with your head up, looking to the hills from which all of your help comes. Sometimes it gets so hard, and it seems that God has forgotten all about you. I want to serve notice to you, God has not forgotten you. Habakkuk 2:3 tells us… "*there is a time set for the deliverance of God's people, that will come, though it seems to tarry; and when it comes, it will appear to have been the best time and therefore we ought to wait for it.*"

We need to be patient and faint not; the Word tells us to not be weary in well doing. Joseph stayed in prison for thirteen years until the time that His word came. Those that wait patiently for God will be paid for their waiting (Isaiah 40:31).

You've asked God to enlarge your territory … He heard you.

You've asked God to order your steps … He heard you.

You've prayed and you've cried … He heard you.

Yes, God heard every groan, now this is your time and the wait is over. The fullness has come, now it's time to walk into your season. Remember all those seeds that you've sown? Well, it's reaping time. God is going to fulfil every promise He made to you because what God has for you is for you … you need to send up Judah right here. Hallelujah.

Yes, Satan is going to attack you, but you will be able to stand because God is in control. Don't fear, just walk into your season. God is taking you to the next level, just tell the Lord, "*Yes!*" The Bible says to resist the devil, and he will flee (James 4:7). Yes, the enemy will try to pull you back, just say, "***In the Name of Jesus*** *I command you Satan to get out of my way.*" Yes, you have that authority. Who are you? Just say, "*I am a Blood washed Sanctified Holy Ghost filled child of God, I am who God says I am so therefore I am going to walk into my season because I know that God has not forgotten.*"

Declare today…

Satan you can't have my home; I'm taking it back.

You can't have my husband; I'm taking it back.

You can't have my mind; I'm taking it back.

You can't have my children; I'm taking it back.

I'm walking into my season of miracles, into my season of plenty, season of joy, peace, faith, love and happiness; this is my season in the name of Jesus! The favor of God is upon my life so therefore I'm going to recover all. Hallelujah! I know that God is on my side, and He won't let me down because I've got that promise. Whatever I need is in the name of Jesus. He is my all in all, He is my bread when I am hungry, my water when I'm thirsty, He is my healer, counselor, my Jehovah Jireh, Jehovah Rophi, Jehovah Nissi. God said it, He has ordained it and I accept it in the name of Jesus.

We need to understand that the reason we go through a lot of the things we go through is because Satan sees where God is taking you. He's trying to stop you because of where you are going in Christ. So, make up in your mind that whatever it takes you are going to receive what God has in store for you. Don't let the devil discourage you; stand still, stop running and see the salvation of the Lord this is your time (2 Chronicles 20:17). God has great things in store for you. Don't you know that you are of greatness? God has a plan for your life and the enemy knows that. That's why he's trying so hard to stop and block you. Don't let him, step on the devils' head while you are stepping into your season.

Sometimes things may not work the way we think they should but stay in the race and keep a steady pace. Your steps have been ordered. The race is not given to the swift nor to the strong but to the one that endures to the end. There is a great reward for you if you just stand. Praise God!!! God has got better for you because you are of royalty. Don't you know that you are of a royal priesthood? You deserve the best and you shouldn't settle for less.

Remember Joseph was in captivity from the time he was seventeen until he was thirty, but he never gave up. He endured all the humiliation and the suffering that he was put through (2 Timothy 2:3-5). So don't you give up either, you are about to walk into your wealthy place. God has made good on His promise. I am encouraged to go all the way with the Lord because I can't remember how it feels to be anywhere, but where I am right now. Glory to God, because I've stepped into my season. Job 11:16 says, "*Because thou shall forget thy misery, and remember it as waters that pass away.*"

We love God, not just because of what He has done but because of who He is. One day I want to see Him face to face because He will wipe away all my tears. There will be no more heartaches, no more pain in my body, no more humiliation, no more being lied on, no more being accused… Hallelujah. All my troubles will be no more (1 Corinthians 2:9). I am looking to hear Him say, "*Well done thy good and faithful servant, well done!*"

Two

DRESS CODE

LET'S TALK ABOUT IT

We've gotten so caught up in looking like what we think living **Holy** is all about. But in the term "Dress Code", God is saying; "*But seek ye first the Kingdom of God, and His righteousness; and all these things shall be added unto you,*" Matthew 6:33.

1. How should we dress?
   A. 1 Peter 5:5

   Be clothed with humility: for God resisteth the proud, and giveth grace to the humble.
   Humility is the absence of selfishness and arrogance. One who is humble does not "think of himself more highly than he ought to think". Some are walking around clothed with selfishness and arrogancy but God resisteth the proud and gives grace to the humble. We need to talk off the garment of selfishness and arrogancy and put on the garment of humility and praise. We must humble ourselves before God and realize we are nothing without Him.

   B. Ephesians 6:11-17

   Put on the whole armour of God, that ye may be able to stand against the wiles of the devil.
   For we wrestle not against flesh and blood, but against principalities, against powers, against spiritual wickedness in high places.
   Wherefore take unto you the whole armour of God, that ye may be able to withstand in the evil day, and having done all, to stand.

Stand therefore, having your loins girt about with the truth, and having on the breastplate of righteousness;
And your feet shod with the preparation of the gospel of peace;
Above all, taking the shield of faith, wherewith ye shall be able to quench all the fiery darts of the wicked.
And take the helmet of salvation, and the sword of the spirit, which is the word of God: Putting on the whole armour of God provides spiritual strength, protection, stamina to combat those fiery darts that the devil will throw.

C. Galatians 5:22-23

But the fruit of the Spirit is love, joy, peace, longsuffering, gentleness, goodness, faith, meekness, temperance: against such there is no law.

Let's get back on course. The devil has so many of us focused on the outer garment we've forgotten to dress up the inner man.

There was an episode I watched on television concerning the putting on of a garment. This character was supposedly interested in becoming and living his African roots. He was being coached on what to do, what to wear and even went as far as changing his name. He decided to purchase a Dashiki which he wore thinking he looked like what he was trying to portray. I can imagine he thought he had it going on. After all of this, he thinks, "*This is it, I've arrived, I look like I belong.*" After a while, his coach arrived at his house and observed his interaction with his father. There was something lacking in this alleged transformation. His coach informed him that his behavior and actions were not respectful to his elderly father. The coach advised him that putting on a garment to look like something or someone does not make you genuine. It's in the heart. In other words, it's the inner man that must be changed. When the inner man is changed, I believe we will know how to dress appropriately.

Hosea 4:6 says, "… *my people are destroyed for lack of knowledge*:"

We need to understand that a garment will not save you nor will it send you to hell. The inner man is starving because we are focused on the outer man and what the outer looks like. Stop the insanity, because when we stand before God, our outer garment is not going to be judged. It's in the heart. Make sure the inner man meets criteria.

2. How can you know if you are clothed properly?
   A. 1 Peter 3:3-4

      "**Do not let your adornment be merely outward-arranging the hair, wearing gold, or putting on fine apparel-rather let it be the hidden person of the heart, with the incorruptible beauty of a gentle and quiet spirit, which is very precious in the sight of God**."

As we walk with the Lord, our outer appearance should reflect our identity in Christ. When we clothed ourselves properly, we are not just letting others see what we look like on the outside, but we are affirming who and whose we are. Our garments show our character. We need to dress in a way that honors God and reflect our values.

(Don't show it all Cover it up!)

B. II Corinthians 5:17

Therefore, if any man be in Christ, he is a new creature: old things are passed away; behold, all things are become new.

3. What should we avoid when dressing?

A. Galatians 5:19-21

Now the works of the flesh are manifest, which are these; Adultery, fornication, uncleanness, lasciviousness, idolatry, witchcraft, hatred, variance, emulations, wrath, strife, seditions, heresies, envyings, murders, drunkenness, revellings, and such like: of the which I tell you before, as I have also told you in time past, that they which do such things shall not inherit the kingdom of God.

B. Avoid pridefulness and arrogancy

4. Does what you wear naturally so, make you Holy?

No, it doesn't! First of all, we need to know the meaning of holy.

Holy is dedicated, consecrated to God.

Having a divine quality.

Sacred.

1 Peter 1:16 (read full chapter)

1:16 ... "*Because it is written, Be ye holy; for I am holy.*"

Holiness is moral purity; freedom from sin;

Holiness is a state of being; it's an inside job.

Matthew 23:24-28….

Ye blind guides, which strain at a gnat, and swallow a camel.

> **Woe unto you, scribes and pharisees, hypocrites! For ye make clean the outside of the cup and of the platter, but within they are full of extortion and excess.**
> **Thou blind pharisee, cleanse first that which is within the cup and the platter, that the outside of them may be clean also.**
> **Woe unto you, scribes and pharisees, hypocrites! For ye are like unto whited sepulchres, which indeed appear beautiful outward, but are full of dead men's bones, and uncleanness.**
> **Even so ye also outwardly appear righteous unto men, but within ye are full of hypocrisy and iniquity.**

Dress up the inside with Holiness and Righteousness so that others can see Christ in our lives. It's not about the pants. Some of us are going to miss the mark worrying about who's wearing pants. It's not in the garment; it's in your heart. As I forestated, when the heart is changed, we will know how to dress appropriately. Stop the insanity and let's get our focus back on the assignment that God has given us. **Soul Winning!** Keep on the whole armor of God, so that others can see Christ in our lives by the way we live, serve, give, and worship. But most importantly, live so that God can use us any place and at any time.

Three

“SOMEBODY NEEDS TO STAND”

Some time ago God gave me this topic, "*Somebody needs to stand.*" There was and still is so much corruption going on in this world and yes in our churches. People that are supposedly saved, sanctified, and Holy Ghost filled are doing all sorts of ungodly things. I'm wondering how can this be? Well, the devil has crept in and led a lot of people astray. People are letting the standard of holiness down. They're focusing on material things, worldly pleasures, positions in the churches as well as the government. They've gotten away from true holiness. As I look at the conditions of this world it grieves my heart. If people all around you decide to let the gap down, you maintain and continually stand for righteousness.

As I begin to read Ephesians 6:10-17, I see where Paul was letting the Ephesians know they needed to stand. We must do as Paul instructed the Ephesians; put on the whole armor of God. I believe the reason we see so much unrighteousness is because the whole armor of God is not in place. This is why we see so much hatred and envy among our brothers and sisters in Christ. This is not how God intended us to be. We are to be an example of righteousness. We that are save and are real for Jesus, we need to stand. Paul says, "*…for we wrestle not against flesh and blood, but against principalities, against powers, against the rulers of the darkness of this world, against spiritual wickedness in high places.*" The devil is out to destroy the very elect of God. He is on his job, so we must be aware of his devices. Do you realize all the devil wants is for you to lower your standards. Remember, he is a trickster and a deceiver. That's why we need on the whole armor of God. By having on the whole armor of God, we will be able to stand against the wiles of the devil. If the devil can't get you one way, then he will try another. Remember we are covered by the blood of the Lamb. Get into the Word of God and study. Spend time with God in prayer. Ask God, "*Create in me a clean heart and renew a right spirit in me.*"

All of these things will give you strength in time of adversity. Paul said, "*Wherefore take unto you the whole armor of God, that you may be able to withstand in the evil day, and having done all to stand, stand therefore.*" We as saints of God are to draw others to Christ by the way we walk and live. Are we walking and living according to the will of God? Are we turning our backs and closing our eyes on the things that are going on in our churches today? We need to **wake up**, **get up,** and **stand up**. We need to stop letting any and everything go in in our midst. It is wrong for the preacher to have affairs with the members in his church. It is wrong for the deacons to steal the money from the church. Just as it is wrong for the leaders to commit adultery, it is equally wrong for the woman or man to submit to the advances. All unrighteousness is sin! **Somebody needs to stand.** When you see something, you need to say something. We've been sitting quietly for too long.

I had a dream one night that the founder of our church, Bishop C.H. Mason, was turning over in his grave. This was very disturbing to me. I hadn't ever dreamed of Bishop Mason before. I called a man of God to interpret this dream. Too much is going on in our churches so it's time for us to cry aloud and spare not (Isaiah 58:1).

We can't continually sit by and say nothing. We must speak what God has given us to speak. It's time to raise the standard of holiness. Let us seek the old path. I used to hear my grandmother say, "*We need to go back to the old landmark.*" I know now what she was talking about. She was not talking about going back to the cotton fields nor was she talking about going back to the horse and buggy. She was talking about holiness. Jeremiah 6:16…we need to stand in the ways, and see, and ask for the old paths, (but there are many that are saying, "*We will not walk therein.*"). We need to go back to letting our "Yea" be "Yea" and our "Nay" be "Nay." I see so many acting like they don't know what true holiness is. True holiness is living a sin free life according to the will of God. True holiness is loving like the Bible instructs. I agree with my grandmother, we need to go back. Again, it's time to raise the standard of holiness. It's time to stop preaching on Sunday mornings and tipping on Sunday evening. It's time to take a stand against unrighteousness. If your brother or sister feel they need to slip and tip, then you stand. Just because there is corruption in your midst, you do not have to succumb to the devil. The Bible tells us to resist the devil, and he will flee. The Lord is depending on us to be an example of holiness.

Do not be concerned when people turn their back on you because you are speaking the truth and calling out their sins. You just stand because you have an assignment to deliver what God has given you.

So, through the fiery darts, **stand**! Through the trials, **stand**! Stand for holiness. You be the one that makes a difference. Remember God is depending on us to be an example. Can He depend on you to say "Yes" to what is right? It does not matter, from the pulpit to the back door; all unrighteousness is sin. Are you going to go along with wrong or will you **stand** in the midst of corruption for what is right? You can't stop people from doing wrong, but you can be a righteous example. Stay in the word of God and keep that close communion with Him. Have your loins girt about with truth and have on the breastplate of righteousness and your feet shod with the preparation of the gospel of peace, above all, taking the shield of faith, wherewith you shall be able to quench all the fiery darts of the wicked. And take the helmet of salvation, and the sword of the spirit, which is the Word of God. Are you encouraged to stand for what is right realizing God sees all and He knows all? Proverbs 15:3… "*the eyes of the Lord are in every place, beholding the evil and the good.*"

I'm encouraged to stand for what is right because I know that one day I must leave here going to a better place. A place where there will be no more pain, a place where trouble will be no more, Glory to God! There will be no more tears, no more being lied on and lied to, no more being criticized or talked about. God Himself is going to wipe away all of my tears, Hallelujah!!!! I'm living to live again with Jesus. I want to hear Him say, "*Well done thy good and faithful servant.*" What do you want the Lord to say? Do you want to hear Him say, "*Well done thou good and faithful servant*"? Well, to hear this, we must continue to stand for righteousness. Will you stand with me? Let's stand together. One can put a thousand to flight and two can put ten thousand to flight (Deuteronomy 32:30).

Let's go back to that old landmark and …

LET THE HEALING BEGIN!

Four

DON'T GIVE UP, GOD IS POSITIONING YOU TO RECEIVE

This topic brings to mind a song my grandparents sang. "My Lord's gettin' us ready for that great day, who shall be able to stand?" In this life we will encounter ups and downs, we don't know exactly why, but God knows (Jeremiah 29:11).

As we look at the word **position**, we understand that it means preparing for a specific task or duty. In other words, "*Get ready, get ready, get ready.*" God is getting you in position to receive; yes, God is about to blow your mind. (Glory to God!)

Let's talk about a woman of God that did not give up, she was one that looked to God and trusted Him because she knew He would not fail her. You'll find her in the book of 1 Samuel 1:9-20. Yes, I'm talking about Hannah. She was a woman of faith that endured some real problems: her womb was closed, she was constantly provoked by her rival Peninnah and the priest Eli thought she was drunken. Hannah endured a lot because there was something she was looking for from God. Remember the song, "My Lord's getting' us ready for that great day, who shall be able to stand?" God was getting her in position to receive. Through her trials and difficult times, Hannah continued to pray fervently to God (James 5:16c). It didn't matter how foolish she may have looked to Eli, she continued to pray, she didn't give up, she stayed the course. In other words, she pursued regardless of the obstacles and regardless of the criticism. It doesn't matter how others may view you, keep coming to the altar and count it all joy; know that God is getting you ready to receive that you've been seeking. Hannah wanted a child, but she had to be in the right position. We must be in the right mindset to receive; a mind-set of praise, obedience, trust, and tenacity. Hannah was taunted and provoked by another woman's malice, but she refused to stoop to Peninnah's level of evil. The devil will want to take you there but let me encourage you: don't give up. Continue to trust in God and stay the course. Hannah stood for a long time at the tabernacle weeping and praying, her lips moved without making a sound as her heart poured out grief unto the Lord. She cried; "O Lord Almighty remember me your servant." You have cried but remember God sees and He knows all, count it all joy because God is getting you ready to receive your healing, breakthrough, peace. You may have been cast down but not destroyed.

James says, "*Count it all joy!*" Everything you went through was for your good and for God's Glory. Hannah was in position and received her child. There's a song that says, "*Got just what I wanted from the Lord.*" God is getting us ready to be able to stand against the wiles of the devil. God is getting us ready to receive. Just as Hannah received because she didn't give up, she endured hardness as a good soldier. She was persistent in her prayer unto God. To the reader of this topic: Get ready, get ready, get ready, get in position. Glory to God! God is getting ready to do exceedingly abundantly above all we can ask or think (Ephesians 3:20). There may be some contrary winds that blow but stay the course. Stay the course when you arc tircd of the battle, stay the course when it doesn't feel good. Because to receive and finish well we must be committed to staying the course.

We must understand that our steps have been ordered by God. Just trust the process. Just as Hannah had to go through the process to receive, we must go through as well. Although various trials and afflictions, hardships, difficulties may come, we need to hold on because God knows what's best for us. So many times, we want to step over or skip the process because we don't like how the process feels but stay the course. God has ordered your steps. Sometimes we want to bypass the process but that may be the very moment you need to develop patience, peace, and endurance. God has a plan for all of us. Glory to God! Stop trying to go around the plan that is set for you because God is taking you somewhere.

During the step process you may have to encounter the step of being lied on, people turning their back on you, being lied too, being cast aside, discouragement and even disappointment but count it all joy and know that it's working for your good.

Hannah was a prime example of someone that didn't give up and received what God had for her.

In your leisure read about how Joseph was positioned by God to go from the pit to the palace (Genesis chapters 37-50).

Also read how God positioned a little orphan girl and made her a Queen (The Book of Esther).

God has greatness in store for you. Although Hannah was provoked, God positioned her to receive. Although Joseph was hated by his half-brothers, God positioned him to receive. Although Esther was a little orphan girl (some say was born on the wrong side of the tracks), God positioned her to receive. When God has His Hand on you no one can stop you from getting what God has in store for you. HALLELUJAH!!

So don't give up. God is calling you to a higher place in Him. God is getting ready to place you before great men (Proverbs 18:16).

Get ready, God is opening doors that man thought they had closed (Revelation 3:8).

Get ready, God is bringing that wayward child home. He is healing, delivering, and setting the captive free (Glory to God!).

Don't give up, we've got just a few more risings and settings of the sun.

Now receive what God has for you!

LET THE HEALING BEGIN!

Five

DO YOU HEAR THE WORDS…

THAT ARE COMING OUT OF YOUR MOUTH?

"Let the words of my mouth, and the meditation of my heart, be acceptable in thy sight, O Lord, my strength, and my redeemer." (Psalm 19:14)

Oftentimes we recite that particular scripture passage before we bring a message or during greetings to a congregation. Yes, the Word is powerful but are we reciting it with sincerity or reciting it because it sounds good? Let's look at; "Let the words of my mouth be acceptable."

Do you hear the words that are coming out of your mouth? Are they words of encouragement, uplifting, praise and adoration? Are they words of criticism or hatred? Are they words of gloom and despair and agony, deep dark depression and excessive misery? We need to be mindful of the words spoken from our mouths. Sometimes we think we are doing people a favor when we are supposedly speaking into their lives. If we are not speaking from a pure heart, then it profits nothing. First, make sure that our words are acceptable in the sight of God. Pray as David did; "*Create in me a clean heart O God; and renew a right spirit within me* (Psalm 51:10) *because I want my words to be acceptable in thy sight."*

Remember that our words have power … Proverbs 18:21a tells us, "*Death and Life are in the power of the tongue.*" So, you see we can speak life, or we can speak death. Which one are we speaking?

I Peter 3:10 … It is important to keep your tongue from evil and lips from deceitful speech. When you use your mouth to speak things that are deceitful and evil, do you know that you can possibly break up someone's home or even your own home? Speaking the wrong words can possibly cause someone to lose their life or may cause you to lose yours. Be mindful of what you say.

Remember that our ultimate goal is to please God. We've said, "*Let the words of my mouth be acceptable.*" Are our words pleasing to God or sounding like brass or tinkling cymbals? In other words, are we talking loudly and saying nothing? Do our words have merit? Are we just speaking to impress? Remember, God sees all, hears all, and knows all. Have you ever planted a garden and watched it grow? Whatever the seed, you expected it to grow into something spectacular. Our words are like seeds, once you've planted them, they will grow; more than likely they will grow into something good or something bad. Be careful of the seeds you plant. I've heard some young parents telling their children, "*You are no good, you're lazy, you're crazy, you're ugly.*" Stop the insanity and start speaking favor over your children, because surely one day those seeds will take root.

Growing up as a child in the South, I was reared in a God-Fearing home. I learned to work for a living, I had to go to church, respect my elders, and so on. My grandparents, the late Elder Tom Collins and the late Mother Mary J. Collins, planted seeds of righteousness with clean living. Proverbs 22:6 says, "*Train up a child in the way he should go: and when he is old, he will not depart from it.*" Praise God for the seeds they planted. Thank God the seeds took root. Glory To God!!! Let's plant the proper seeds.

Psalm 19:14 goes on to say, "*and the meditation of my heart.*"

What are you meditating on? If you ponder in your heart gloom and despair, gloom and despair will come from your mouth. It doesn't matter how much you say, "*I love you,*" if it's not in your heart, it won't mean much coming out of your mouth. Yes, the real you will show up.

Matthew 15:18a tells us, "*But those things which proceed out of the mouth comes forth from the heart;*"

Matthew 15:19 says, "*For out of the heart proceed evil thoughts, murders, adulteries, fornication, thefts, false witness, blasphemies.*" That's what happens when you are outside the will of God, you begin to meditate on the wrong things. This is why we need on the whole armor of God. Remember, the safest place in the whole wide world is in the will of God.

I'm reminded of the story of David and his infidelity as he lusted in his heart for Uriah's wife. He spotted Bathsheba bathing and despite her marital status, he sent for her. This is what David was meditating on. He went as far as having her husband killed trying to cover up his wrongdoing. He had a heart problem. He was meditating on the wrong thing. But David realized he had messed up and wanted to get it right before God. Some of us have a heart problem. Don't just sit idle letting the enemy play with your mind. That's all he wants is a playground. If you allow him access, he will have you meditating on all the wrong things.

Then once you've meditated for a while, the enemy will convince you to act on the thing you've been meditating on. We need to do as David says in Psalm 51:10…. "*Create in me a clean heart O God; and renew a right spirit within me*"; we need to cry out – "*Lord, I'm meditating on the wrong things, and I need your help. I want the mediation of my heart to be acceptable in your sight.*" If we are sincere, God will come to our rescue because He is a very present help in a time of trouble; HALLELUJAH!!!!

Philippians 4:8 … "*Finally, brethren, whatsoever things are true, whatsoever things are honest, whatsoever things are lovely, whatsoever things are of good report; if there be any virtue, and if there be any praise, think on these things.*"

When we think of the goodness of Jesus and all He has done for us, perfect praise will begin to come forth, because the more we praise, the more we want to praise; HALLELUJAH!!!

So, you see the more you meditate on Jesus, the more praise and encouragement come from your heart, thus coming from your mouth. We must be mindful of the things that are coming from our mouths and …

Six

KEEP IT UNDER CONTROL

YOUR TEMPLE!

1 Corinthians 6:19-20 … "*What? Know ye not that your body is the temple of the Holy Ghost, which is in you, which ye have of God, and ye are not your own? For ye are bought with a price: therefore, glorify God in your body, and in your spirit, which are God's.*"

I'm a witness that God will keep whatever you place before Him. Try it!

Our bodies are sacred and should be treated with reverence as they are a dwelling place of the Holy Ghost. We can't put any and everything in this temple that God has given us. So many of us have conditions that we have caused ourselves. High blood pressure, obesity, and high cholesterol just to name a few. We eat the wrong things repeatedly. We sometimes don't know how to eat in moderation on the natural side. When the doctor tells us that eating too much fried food everyday will drive that blood pressure up as well as the cholesterol, we tend to turn a deaf ear. The doctor informs us that not cutting back on these types of food will destroy the body, the kidneys may fail, the joints may wear out because of obesity, and that the feet will swell. But we continually disobey the doctor by putting too much of the wrong things in our bodies therefore, destroying the physical body.

God wants us healthy! 3 John 1:2 … "*Beloved, I wish above all things that thou mayest prosper and be in health, even as thy soul prospereth.*"

Our soul will prosper when we feed our temple with the things of the Lord. We must put on the whole armor of God. Spiritually, we can't live any kind of way and think our soul will prosper. We must live according to the will of God. Partaking in the wrong things - such as idolatry, hatred, fornication just to name a few, will cause destruction morally. Know ye not, that your temple is a dwelling place of the Holy Ghost? He will not dwell in an unclean temple. In order to prosper in the things of the Lord, we must be obedient to the Word of God. Just as we must be mindful as to what we put in our bodies naturally so, we must also be mindful what we put in our bodies spiritually so as well. Let's eat more fruit (Galatians 5:22-23), this will do our soul good.

CONTROL YOUR TEMPLE!

Galatians 5:19-21 … "*Now the works of the flesh are manifest, which are these; Adultery, fornication, uncleanness, lasciviousness, idolatry, witchcraft, hatred, variance, emulations, wrath, strife, seditions, heresies, envyings, murders, drunkenness, revellings. Stay away from these things.*"

Men and women, you must learn to control your vessel. Learn to; (1). Trust God (2). Be prayerful. (3). Stop falling for every lie the devil tells you. Don't let the devil deceive you as he did Eve; that's his job. He wants you to fall into the trap of sin. Because he knows if you do, you won't have a keeper. Because as I've stated already, the Holy Ghost (our Keeper) cannot and will not dwell in an unclean temple.

You can be kept by the power of the Holy Ghost.

Sometimes, you may find yourself at the door of temptation, but if you have a made-up mind to bypass that door, you will be victorious. BUT GOD! You can't hang around fire and not be burned. The Devil is a liar and all he wants is for you to disobey the Word of God and fall. He wants to tarnish your character by any means necessary.

1 Thess. 4:3-4 … "*For this is the will of God, even your sanctification, that ye should abstain from fornication. That every one of you should know how to possess his vessel in sanctification and honour.*"

We need to take control of our temple, but we can't do it without the help of God. Ephesians 6:11… "*Put on the whole armor of God and you will be able to resist the enemy.*" Remember, the devil (the enemy) wants you destroyed but we must stand on the word of God; having fastened on the belt of truth, we must have on the breastplate of righteousness to guard our hearts and souls from moral decay.

Psalm 104:4 … "*Seek the Lord, and His strength: seek His face evermore.*" Control your temple, put in more love, joy, peace, longsuffering, gentleness, goodness, faith, meekness and temperance (Gal. 5: 22-23). I repeat … yes, we need to eat more fruit (FRUIT OF THE SPIRIT).

Ways to control your temple:

1. Seek God through prayer, praise, and studying His Word.
2. Place that issue in God's hands (2 Timothy 1:12b).
3. Flee (run) from those things that go against the Word of God (1 Cor. 6:18a, Gen. 39:12).
4. Fast and pray (Mark 9:29)!
5. Pray without ceasing (1 Thess. 5:17).
6. Commit thy way unto the Lord (Psalm 37:5).

KEEP YOUR TONGUE UNDER CONTROL!

What you say can mean LIFE or DEATH. Proverbs 18:21a … "*Death and life are in the power of the tongue.*"

Be mindful of what you say. That little member behind your teeth can tear up some stuff if it gets loose. It can and will destroy families if it gets loose. It can and will cause someone to lose their life if it gets loose. One of my former pastors, the Late Supt. J.B. Harrell, once alluded to this fact. Your teeth are very important, they are there for a reason - not only to chew, but to clamp down and be a cage so that wagging tongue can't get loose. Try it sometime!

James 3:5-8 … "*even so the tongue is a little member, and boasteth great things. Behold, how great a matter a little fire kindleth! And the tongue is a fire, a world of iniquity; so is the tongue among our members, that it defileth the whole body, and setteth on fire the course of nature; and it is set on fire of hell. For every kind of beast, and of birds, and serpents, and of things in the sea, is tamed, and hath been tamed of mankind: but the tongue can no man tame; it is an unruly evil, full of deadly poison.*"

Have you ever been around someone that just talked all the time? They talk about things they know, things they think they know, and they talk about things they've heard. This is a dangerous person. The scripture says, "*study to be quiet*". Let's not be a blabbermouth. People will hate to see you coming. They will say, here comes the blabbermouth. **Get that tongue under control!!**

Here is a list of things that unruly member between those teeth will produce:

Bragging, boastfulness, insults, malice, busy body rumors, back biting, negativity, harassment, arrogancy, name calling, threats, pridefulness, slandering, degrading, gossiping, anger.

Proverbs 21:23 … "*Whoever guards his mouth, and his tongue keeps his SOUL from troubles.*"

Do you know you can talk your way out of a blessing? Some of us talk too much.

1 Thess. 4:11 … "*And that ye study to be quiet, and to do your own business, and to work with your own hands, as we commanded you;*"

1 Peter 3:10-11 … "*For he that will love life, and see good days, let him refrain his tongue from evil. And his lips that speak no guile: let him eschew evil and do good; let him seek peace and ensue it.*"

Guard your tongue, get it under control by putting on the whole armor of God.

James 4:7 … "*Submit yourselves therefore to God. Resist the devil, and he will flee from you.*"

<u>KEEP YOUR CONDUCT (BEHAVIOR) UNDER CONTROL!</u>

Be mindful of your conduct, the way you act and behave. Remember, your ATTITUDE determines your ALTITUDE.

Conduct can be ORDERLY or DISORDERLY.

Orderly behaviors maintain controls and disorderly behavior engages in unreasonable noise and disruptive behavior. Do you realize that when you say you are saved and sold out to Christ, the world is watching you? Well, to draw others to Christ, we must live what we profess. 2 Corinthians 3: 2 says, "*Ye are our epistle written in our hearts, known and read of all men.*"

I know that sometimes things don't go our way and this can cause us to become upset. Ephesians 4:26 … "*Be ye angry and sin not.*" While it is natural to feel angry, you should not let that anger lead to sin and cause you to lose control. Pray and ask God for help. Psalm 46:1 … "*God is our refuge and strength, a very present help in trouble.*"

Here are a few scriptures to help in controlling your behavior:

Galatians 5:22-23 - EAT MORE FRUIT

2 Peter 1:5-7, James 1:19-20, 1 Peter 1:13-16, Titus 2:11-12, 2 Timothy 1:7 Proverbs 25:28, Proverbs 16:32

As I stated earlier, the world is watching us; whether it's on our job, in our community, in our homes, or in our churches, yes, we are being watched. That lost promotion on your job may have been caused by your ATTITUDE. GET IT UNDER CONTROL! One of the older mothers in our church once stated, "*The way you live after the benediction will determine your destination.*" SO, GET IT UNDER CONTROL! You may have failed in leading someone to Christ because of your ATTITUDE. GET IT UNDER CONTROL! Remember, you are not "all that." Some of us think we are "all that and a bag of chips." Remember God hates a proud look (Proverbs 6:17a).

Controlling your conduct in your Christian walk is very important. It is a divine attribute, cultivated by the Holy Ghost, that helps you to live in a manner worthy of your calling. We all have choices, let's choose to be kind, choose to seek God, and choose to trust God. We want to please God and hear Him say, "*Well done good and faithful servant.*"

Seven

BOAZ WAS THERE ALL THE TIME

Ask yourself these questions! Has Boaz been in my life all the time? Have I been waiting on Boaz? Have I been looking for Boaz? Some of us have been living with Boaz but we didn't realize it. Notice, I said **some of us**. Attractions, distractions, and infractions have caused some of us to lose sight of our very own Boaz.

Let's first take a look at these three words:

(1) **Attraction:** the action or power of evoking interest, pleasure, or liking for someone or something; a quality or feature that evokes interest liking of desire.

(2) **Distraction:** A thing that prevents someone from giving full attention to someone or something; a diversion (diverting one's attention).

(3) **Infraction**: A violation or infringement of a law or agreement; the breaking of a law(covenant) rule or agreement.

Yes, these three (attraction, distraction and infraction) have caused many of us to lose out on our very own Boaz. Think about the role Boaz played in the book of Ruth. Boaz played an important role as Kinsman-Redeemer, demonstrating kindness, integrity and fulfillment of God's law through his relationship with Ruth and Naomi. According to the Jewish law, a Kinsman-Redeemer had the responsibility to **Protect** and **Provide**. Boaz was a gentleman, kind, humble, and considerate. He put Ruth's needs before his own; You see, he is bold and not afraid to act with purpose. He made special provisions so that Ruth could gather grain in his fields. In other words, Boaz took care of this woman. Can you see these traits in your Boaz? Yes, I said your Boaz. Does he protect and provide for you?

Sometimes we get attracted by other things we feel are better than what we already have. We let social media, soap operas and even other people's lives influence our thinking. This is a trick of the devil, trying to make you believe it could be better than what you've got right now. You see men opening doors for the woman to let her enter first, yes that's admirable, but that doesn't make the man. You may even see them strolling along, hand in hand, again that's admirable but, that doesn't make the man. A lot of what we see is fake. Fake news, fake television. So now we've become attracted to a life that's not real. Now we've become dissatisfied with what we have (keep in mind the role of Boaz). He **Protects** and **Provides**. He might not open your door or hold your hand in public, but he provides. You are not going to get roses every day, you may not ever get roses, but if your Boaz loves you then roses don't matter. Question is, does he protect and provide for you? We must learn to be content (Philippians 4:11). God see and God knows.

Sometimes during discontentment, we let the enemy distract us from seeing that our Boaz is here and doing what he can. Every man is not the same. God has made all men uniquely different yet in His own image.

Sometimes attractions, distractions and infractions will cause your Boaz to forget who he is. Did you give up on your Boaz because these things entered his mind? If your Boaz is a non-believer, **PRAY.** For the unbelieving husband is sanctified by the wife, and the unbelieving wife is sanctified by the husband (1 Corinthians 7:14a); **prayer changes things.**

Another question, did attractions, distractions or infractions enter your mind ultimately causing you to give up on your Boaz? Appreciate Boaz for what he is already doing. Thank God for him and help him be all he can be through prayer. If God saved you, God can and will save him. So don't look over the fence looking for Boaz because all you will see is Bozo. Mind you, someone is probably waiting on the Boaz that you kicked to the curb because of attractions, distractions, and infractions, whether they're yours or his.

Don't be like David in this matter. He let his attraction to Bathsheba cause him to become distracted by the lust of his mind, ultimately causing him to commit an infraction.

Don't let the lust of this world cause you to lose out on what God has in store for you. The devil wants you to miss out by any means necessary. Get your eyes off the things of the world and focus on the things of the Lord. God has blessed you with your very own Boaz so there is no need to look across the field. Take the blinders off and see the realness God has already provided. Don't let your guard down for fake attractions it's only a trick of the devil to try and destroy what God has put together. There will be some disappointments, disagreements and some tears shed, but remember, this is only a part of life. Hold on to your Boaz and let God fix it through prayer. The enemy wants you to fail in your marriage. The devil is a liar! We come against the spirit of attractions, distractions, and infractions in the name of Jesus.

Sidebar: Every man is not a Boaz, nor every man a Bozo.

Now let's pray without ceasing and….

LET THE HEALING BEGIN!

Zoë Life Publishing

Zoë Life Publishing is a publishing imprint that releases titles committed to offering encouragement and that are life transforming. We desire for our titles to impact readers in a way that is beyond entertainment; a way that will bring healing, restoration, or even productivity to one's life.

Scan the QR code with your phone's camera to visit our website today for more information.

www.ingramcontent.com/pod-product-compliance
Lightning Source LLC
LaVergne TN
LVHW010943110826
845149LV00013B/2740

* 9 7 9 8 9 9 2 7 3 6 0 7 6 *